I0448520

DEC. 2011

Test Results for Forensic Media Preparation
Tool: Tableau TDW1 Drive Tool / Drive
Wiper - Firmware version: 04/07/10 18:21:33

NCJ 236222

John Laub
Director, National Institute of Justice

This report was prepared for the National Institute of Justice, U.S. Department of Justice, by the Office of Law Enforcement Standards of the National Institute of Standards and Technology under Interagency Agreement 2003–IJ–R–029.

The National Institute of Justice is a component of the Office of Justice Programs, which also includes the Bureau of Justice Assistance, the Bureau of Justice Statistics, the Office of Juvenile Justice and Delinquency Prevention, and the Office for Victims of Crime.

August 2011

Test Results for Forensic Media Preparation Tool:
Tableau TDW1 Drive Tool / Drive Wiper - Firmware version: 04/07/10
18:21:33

**National Institute of
Standards and Technology**
U.S. Department of Commerce

Contents

Introduction

The Computer Forensics Tool Testing (CFTT) program is a joint project of the National Institute of Justice (NIJ), the Department of Homeland Security, and the National Institute of Standards and Technology's Law Enforcement Standards Office and Information Technology Laboratory. CFTT is supported by other organizations, including the Federal Bureau of Investigation, the U.S. Department of Defense Cyber Crime Center, the U.S. Internal Revenue Service Criminal Investigation Division Electronic Crimes Program, the Bureau of Immigration and Customs Enforcement, U.S. Customs and Border Protection and the U.S. Secret Service. The objective of the CFTT program is to provide measurable assurance to practitioners, researchers and other applicable users that the tools used in computer forensics investigations provide accurate results. Accomplishing this requires the development of specifications and test methods for computer forensics tools and subsequent testing of specific tools against those specifications.

Test results provide the information necessary for developers to improve tools, users to make informed choices, and the legal community and others to understand the tools' capabilities. This approach to testing computer forensic tools is based on well-recognized methodologies for conformance and quality testing. The specifications and test methods are posted on the CFTT Web site (http://www.cftt.nist.gov/) for review and comment by the computer forensics community.

This document reports the results from testing the wipe function of Tableau TDW1 Drive Tool / Drive Wiper - Firmware version 04/07/10 18:21:33 against the *Forensic Media Preparation Tool Test Assertions and Test Plan Version 1.0*, available at the CFTT Web site (http://www.cftt.nist.gov/fmp-atp-pc-01.pdf).

Test results for other devices and software packages using the CFTT tool methodology can be found on NIJ's CFTT Web page, http://www.nij.gov/nij/topics/forensics/evidence/digital/standards/cftt.htm.

How to Read This Report

This report is divided into four sections. The first section is a summary of the results from the test runs. This section is sufficient for most readers to assess the suitability of the tool for its intended use. The remaining sections of the report describe how the tests were conducted and provide documentation of test case details that support the report summary. Section 2 gives the selection of each test case from the set of possible cases defined in the test plan for forensic media preparation tools. The test cases are selected, in general, based on features offered by the tool. Section 3 lists the hardware and software used to run the test cases, with links to additional information about the items used. Section 4 contains a description of each test case, listing all test assertions that apply along with their expected results and the actual results. Please refer to the vendor's Web page (https://www.tableau.com/index.php?pageid=products&model=TDW1) for guidance on using the tool.

Test Results for Forensic Media Preparation Tool

Tool Tested: Tableau TDW1 Drive Tool / Drive Wiper
Version: 04/07/10 18:21:33
Serial Number: 015710CE 1026

Run Environment: Custom

Supplier: Guidance Software, Inc.
                    W223 N608 Saratoga Drive
                    Waukesha, WI 53186

Tel: (262) 522-7890
Fax: (262) 522-7899

WWW: https://www.tableau.com/

1   Results Summary

The Tableau TDW1 Drive Tool / Drive Wiper is a multipurpose tool designed to erase SATA hard drives. It provides single- or multi-pass drive wiping options accessible from a menu-driven interface located on the front panel of the device.

In all the test cases, the Tableau TDW1 Drive Tool / Drive Wiper - version 04/07/10 18:21:33 overwrote all visible sectors successfully.

The tool does not automatically remove hidden sectors from source drives but is designed to alert the user when hidden sectors exist. The user may either leave the hidden sectors as is or manually remove them using the "Disk Utilities" *Remove DCO & HPA* menu option. In cases FMP-03-DCO-2, FMP-03-DCO-HPA-2 and FMP-03-HPA-2, the *Remove DCO & HPA* option was not exercised and hidden sectors were not overwritten. In cases FMP-03-DCO, FMP-03-DCO-HPA and FMP-03-HPA, the *Remove DCO & HPA* option was exercised and all sectors were successfully overwritten.

Table 1 provides a brief overview of the test case results.

Table 1. Overview of Test Results

Test Case	Total Sectors	First Sector Overwritten	Last Sector Overwritten	Unchanged Sectors	
				First	Last
FMP-01-SATA28	78140160	0	78140159		
FMP-01-SATA48	312581808	0	312581807		
FMP-03-DCO	234441648	0	234441647		
FMP-03-DCO-2	390721968	0	380721966	380721967	390721967
FMP-03-DCO-HPA	488397168	0	488397167		
FMP-03-DCO-HPA-2	234441648	0	209441646	209441647	234441647
FMP-03-HPA	156301488	0	156301487		
FMP-03-HPA-2	390721968	0	375721966	375721967	390721967

Test Case Selection

Tableau TDW1 Drive Tool / Drive Wiper was only tested for its ability to overwrite sectors of a disk drive. The overwrite command can be run in either 'single' or 'multiple pass' mode. See the 'Log Highlights' box of Test Details section 4.2 for more details as to the construction of each individual test setup.

The test cases were selected from cases defined by *Forensic Media Preparation Tool Test Assertions and Test Plan Version 1.0* based on features supported by this tool.

Table 2 shows which wipe mode was selected and the initial fill written to disk (hex value). The fill value written by **diskwipe** to initialize the drive is reported in the column labeled **Initial Fill**.

Table 2. Modes and Values

Test Case	Mode	Initial Fill (hex value)
FMP-01-SATA28	Multiple pass	0x24 ('$')
FMP-01-SATA48	Single pass	0x43 ('C')
FMP-03-DCO	Single pass	0x1C
FMP-03-DCO-2	Single pass	0x33 ('3')
FMP-03-DCO-HPA	Multiple pass	0x2C (',')
FMP-03-DCO-HPA-2	Multiple pass	0x1D
FMP-03-HPA	Single pass	0x32 ('2')
FMP-03-HPA-2	Single pass	0x1C

The following source interfaces were used in testing: SATA28 and SATA48.

Test Materials

1.1 Support Software

Several programs were used in the setup and analysis of the test drives. These include **hdat2** (download from http://www.hdat2.com/download.html), **dsumm** (download from http://www.cftt.nist.gov/), **ransum** (download from http://www.cftt.nist.gov/) and **diskwipe** from **FS-TST Release 2.0** (download from http://www.cftt.nist.gov/diskimaging/fs-tst20.zip).

The **hdat2** program is used to create, remove and document hidden areas on a drive.

The **dsumm** program analyzes the content of a hard drive. It produces a summary of disk contents in terms of counts for each byte value present on the drive. For example, if a drive can contain 10GB (19531250 sectors of 512 bytes per sector) and the drive is wiped with zero bytes, then **dsumm** reports 10,000,000,000 zero bytes. The program also prints the first sector found with printable ASCII content.

The **ransum** program examines a hard drive to identify sectors that do not contain the content written to the drive by the **diskwipe** program. The **ransum** output is a list of sector ranges classified as either *overwritten* or *unchanged*.

The **diskwipe** program initializes a hard drive with known content.

1.2 Test Drive Creation

The following steps are used to set up a test drive:

1. The drive is initially filled with known content by the **diskwipe** program from FS-TST. The **diskwipe** program writes the sector address to each sector in both C/H/S and LBA format. The remainder of the sector bytes is set to a constant fill value unique for each drive. Each sector has known unique content after the setup. The fill value is noted in the **diskwipe** tool log file.
2. The **dsumm** program analyzes the drive contents. This documents the content of the drive.
3. If the drive is intended for hidden area tests (FMP-03), either an HPA, a DCO or a DCO with an HPA is created.
4. The drive size after creation of a hidden area is recorded.

1.3 Test Drive Analysis

The following steps are used to analyze a test drive after it has been wiped by the tool under test:

1. The size of the drive is recorded. This determines if the tool changes the size of a hidden area.
2. Any hidden areas still remaining on the drive are removed.
3. The **dsumm** program is run to determine the final content of the drive.
4. The **ransum** program is run to classify sectors as either *overwritten* or *unchanged*.

1.4 Test Drives

Table 3 lists the hard drives used in testing. The column labeled **Test Case** identifies the test case. The column labeled **Model** is the model of the drive as returned by the ATA IDENTIFY DEVICE command. The column labeled **Serial #** is the serial number as returned by the ATA IDENTIFY DEVICE command.

Table 3. Model and Serial Numbers by Test Case

Test Case	Model	Serial #
FMP-01-SATA28	FUJITSU MHW2040BH	K10XT7B278AP
FMP-01-SATA48	ST3160815AS	9RX7Y1DP
FMP-03-DCO	WDC WD1200JD-00GBB0	WD-WMAES2049679
FMP-03-DCO-2	SAMSUNG SP2004C	S07GJ1ULC07896
FMP-03-DCO-HPA	WDC WD2500AAKS-00VSA0	WD-WMART1591607
FMP-03-DCO-HPA-2	Hitachi HTS542512K9SA00	080914BB6200WBKPDL2G
FMP-03-HPA	Hitachi HDS721680PLA380	PVF804Z31NKPSN
FMP-03-HPA-2	Hitachi HTS722020K9SA00	080703DP04A0DTGL80TC

Table 4 lists the drive configurations for hidden sector test cases. The column labeled **Test Case** identifies the test case. The column labeled **Size** is the number of visible sectors on the drive for the test case. The size of the drive, including both visible and hidden sectors, is reported in the column labeled **Total**. The column labeled **Hidden** is the size in sectors of the hidden area.

Table 4. Drive Configurations for Hidden Sector Tests

Test Case	Size	Total	Hidden (DCO+HPA)
FMP-03-DCO	224441647	234441648	10000001
FMP-03-DCO-2	380721967	390721968	10000001
FMP-03-DCO-HPA	463397167	488397168	25000001 (10000001+15000000)
FMP-03-DCO-HPA-2	209441647	234441648	25000001 (10000001+15000000)
FMP-03-HPA	141301487	156301488	15000001
FMP-03-HPA-2	375721967	390721968	15000001

Test Results

The main item of interest for interpreting the test results is determining the conformance of the tool under test with the test assertions. Conformance with each assertion tested by a given test case is evaluated by examining the **Log Highlights** box of the test report details.

1.5 Test Results Report Key

A summary of the actual test results is presented in this report. The following table presents a description of each section of the test report summary.

Heading	Description
First Line:	Test case ID, name and version of tool tested.
Case Summary:	Test case summary from *Forensic Media Preparation Tool Test Assertions and Test Plan Version 1.0*.
Assertions:	The test assertions applicable to the test case, selected from *Forensic Media Preparation Tool Test Assertions and Test Plan Version 1.0*.
Tester Name:	Name or initials of person executing test procedure.
Analysis Host:	Host used to set up test drive and analyze final drive state.
Test Host:	Host computer executing the test.
Test Date:	Time and date that test was started.

Heading	Description
Test Drive:	Drive erased by the tool under test.
Source Setup:	Report of the native drive size, the size of any hidden areas, the apparent size of the drive (as reported by an ATA IDENTIFY DEVICE command) and an analysis of initial drive contents.
Tool Settings:	Report of tool parameters set for each test run.
Log Highlights:	Report of the state of the drive after executing the tool under test, including the apparent drive size, size of hidden area and analysis of drive contents. The ASCII content of the first non-binary-zero sector is reported.
Results:	Expected and actual results for each assertion tested.
Analysis:	Whether or not the expected results were achieved.

1.6 Test Details

1.6.1 FMP-01-SATA28

Test Case FMP-01-SATA28 Tableau TDW1 F/W version: 04/07/10 18:21:33	
Case Summary:	FMP-01. Overwrite visible sectors using WRITE commands.
Assertions:	FMP-CA-01 All visible sectors shall be overwritten with the specified benign data.
Tester Name:	jrr
Analysis host:	frank
Test host:	tdw1
Test date:	Mon May 16 11:19:34 2011
Test drive:	24-LAP

Source Setup:	Initial setup size: 78140160 from total of 78140160 (with 0 hidden)
	IDE disk: Model (FUJITSU MHW2040BH) serial # (K10XT7B278AP)
	
	Sector 0 is first sector with printable text
	============= Start text =============
	00000/000/01 000000000000$$$
	$$$
	$$$
	$$$
	$$$
	$$$
	$$$
	$$$
	$$$$$$$$$$$$$$$$$$$$$$$$$$$$$$$$$
	============= End text Sector 0 =============
	9 <new line> characters inserted for readability
	
	Totals for all sectors
	summary format: <count> <hex value> <(actual character if printable)> ...
	   78140160 00 78140160 20 ( ) 37976117760 24 ($)
	  156280320 2F (/) 561878293 30 (0) 173598093 31 (1)
	  159768433 32 (2) 142914673 33 (3) 139463608 34 (4)
	  123744696 35 (5) 114674216 36 (6) 107788836 37 (7)
	   98210496 38 (8) 97042176 39 (9)
	Totals for non-ASCII sectors
	summary format: <count> <hex value> <(actual character if printable)> ...
	
	40007761920 bytes, 78140160 sectors, 14 distinct values seen
	78140160 sectors have printable text

Log Highlights:	Size after tool runs: 78140160 from total of 78140160 (with 0 hidden) Analysis of tool result -- Totals for all sectors

```
summary format: <count> <hex value> <(actual character if printable)> ...
 40007761920 FF
Totals for non-ASCII sectors
summary format: <count> <hex value> <(actual character if printable)> ...
 40007761920 FF

40007761920 bytes, 78140160 sectors, 1 distinct values seen
No sectors have printable text


      Runs of Sectors Unchanged or Overwritten
First Sector      Last Sector      State
          0 --       78140159   Overwritten
```

Results:	Assertion & Expected Result	Actual Result	
	FMP-CA-01 Visible sectors overwritten	as expected	
Analysis:	Expected results achieved		

1.6.2 FMP-01-SATA48

Test Case FMP-01-SATA48 Tableau TDW1 F/W version: 04/07/10 18:21:33	
Case Summary:	FMP-01. Overwrite visible sectors using WRITE commands.
Assertions:	FMP-CA-01 All visible sectors shall be overwritten with the specified benign data.
Tester Name:	jrr
Analysis host:	frank
Test host:	twd1
Test date:	Tue May 17 09:06:04 2011
Test drive:	43-SATA

Source Setup:	Initial setup size: 312581808 from total of 312581808 (with 0 hidden)
	IDE disk: Model (ST3160815AS) serial # (9RX7Y1DP)
	
	Sector 0 is first sector with printable text
	============= Start text =============
	00000/000/01 000000000000CCCCCCCCCCCCCCCCCCCCCCCCCCCCCCCCCCCC
	CCCCCCCCCCCCCCCCCCCCCCCCCCCCCCCCCCCCCCCCCCCCCCCCCCCCCCCCCCCCC
	CCCCCCCCCCCCCCCCCCCCCCCCCCCCCCCCCCCCCCCCCCCCCCCCCCCCCCCCCCCCC
	CCCCCCCCCCCCCCCCCCCCCCCCCCCCCCCCCCCCCCCCCCCCCCCCCCCCCCCCCCCCC
	CCCCCCCCCCCCCCCCCCCCCCCCCCCCCCCCCCCCCCCCCCCCCCCCCCCCCCCCCCCCC
	CCCCCCCCCCCCCCCCCCCCCCCCCCCCCCCCCCCCCCCCCCCCCCCCCCCCCCCCCCCCC
	CCCCCCCCCCCCCCCCCCCCCCCCCCCCCCCCCCCCCCCCCCCCCCCCCCCCCCCCCCCCC
	CCCCCCCCCCCCCCCCCCCCCCCCCCCCCCCCCCCCCCCCCCCCCCCCCCCCCCCCCCCCC
	CCCCCCCCCCCCCCCCCCCCCCCCCCCC
	============= End text Sector 0 =============
	9 <new line> characters inserted for readability
	
	Totals for all sectors
	summary format: <count> <hex value> <(actual character if printable)> ...
	  312581808 00 312581808 20 ( ) 625163616 2F (/)
	  1850492169 30 (0) 906528227 31 (1) 696435016 32 (2)
	   541016511 33 (3) 522787395 34 (4) 514450557 35 (5)
	   478352540 36 (6) 458495114 37 (7) 458481159 38 (8)
	   449761088 39 (9) 151914758688 43 (C)
	Totals for non-ASCII sectors
	summary format: <count> <hex value> <(actual character if printable)> ...
	
	160041885696 bytes, 312581808 sectors, 14 distinct values seen
	312581808 sectors have printable text

Tool Settings:	passes: single

Log Highlights:	Size after tool runs: 312581808 from total of 312581808 (with 0 hidden)
	Analysis of tool result --
	Totals for all sectors
	summary format: <count> <hex value> <(actual character if printable)> ...
	160041885696 00
	Totals for non-ASCII sectors
	summary format: <count> <hex value> <(actual character if printable)> ...
	160041885696 00
	
	160041885696 bytes, 312581808 sectors, 1 distinct values seen
	No sectors have printable text
	
	   Runs of Sectors Unchanged or Overwritten
	First Sector Last Sector State
	      0 -- 312581807 Overwritten

Results:	**Assertion & Expected Result** / **Actual Result**
	FMP-CA-01 Visible sectors overwritten | as expected
Analysis:	Expected results achieved

1.6.3 FMP-03-DCO

Test Case FMP-03-DCO Tableau TDW1 F/W version: 04/07/10 18:21:33	
Case Summary:	FMP-03. Overwrite hidden sectors using WRITE commands.
Assertions:	FMP-CA-01 All visible sectors shall be overwritten with the specified benign data. FMP-AO-01 If there is a hidden area present and the tool supports overwriting sectors contained in a hidden area, then all sectors contained in the hidden area shall be overwritten with the specified benign data. FMP-AO-02 A hidden area may optionally be removed from the storage device.
Tester Name:	jrr
Analysis host:	frank
Test host:	tdw1
Test date:	Wed May 18 09:09:59 2011
Test drive:	1C-SATA

Source Setup:	Size with DCO: 224441647 114.91 GB (10000001 sectors in DCO)
	Initial setup size: 224441647 from total of 234441648 (with 10000001 hidden)
	IDE disk: Model (WDC WD1200JD-00GBB0) serial # (WD-WMAES2049679)
	
	Sector 0 is first sector with printable text
	============= Start text =============
	00000/000/01 000000000000
	============= End text Sector 0 =============
	1 \<new line\> character inserted for readability
	
	Totals for all sectors
	summary format: \<count\> \<hex value\> \<(actual character if printable)\> ...
	  224441647 00 109078640442 1C 224441647 20 ( )
	  448883294 2F (/) 1412016103 30 (0) 648943728 31 (1)
	  464424108 32 (2) 386665413 33 (3) 366881139 34 (4)
	  361115513 35 (5) 335339465 36 (6) 320942104 37 (7)
	  320928507 38 (8) 320460154 39 (9)
	Totals for non-ASCII sectors
	summary format: \<count\> \<hex value\> \<(actual character if printable)\> ...
	
	114914123264 bytes, 224441647 sectors, 14 distinct values seen
	224441647 sectors have printable text

Tool Settings:	passes: single option: remove hidden sectors

Log Highlights:	Size after tool runs: 234441648 from total of 234441648 (with 0 hidden)
	Analysis of tool result --
	Totals for all sectors
	summary format: \<count\> \<hex value\> \<(actual character if printable)\> ...
	120034123776 00
	Totals for non-ASCII sectors
	summary format: \<count\> \<hex value\> \<(actual character if printable)\> ...
	120034123776 00
	
	120034123776 bytes, 234441648 sectors, 1 distinct values seen
	No sectors have printable text
	
	    Runs of Sectors Unchanged or Overwritten
	First Sector Last Sector State
	        0 -- 234441647 Overwritten

Results:	Assertion & Expected Result	Actual Result	
	FMP-CA-01 Visible sectors overwritten	as expected	
	FMP-AO-01 Hidden sectors overwritten	as expected	
	FMP-AO-02 Hidden area final state is	removed	
Analysis:	Expected results achieved		

1.6.4 FMP-03-DCO-2

Test Case FMP-03-DCO-2 Tableau TDW1 F/W version: 04/07/10 18:21:33	
Case Summary:	FMP-03. Overwrite hidden sectors using WRITE commands.
Assertions:	FMP-CA-01 All visible sectors shall be overwritten with the specified benign data. FMP-AO-01 If there is a hidden area present and the tool supports overwriting sectors contained in a hidden area, then all sectors contained in the hidden area shall be overwritten with the specified benign data. FMP-AO-02 A hidden area may optionally be removed from the storage device.
Tester Name:	jrr
Analysis host:	frank
Test host:	tdw1
Test date:	Thu May 19 09:21:53 2011
Test drive:	33-SATA

Source Setup:	Size with DCO: 380721967 194.93 GB (10000001 sectors in DCO)
	Initial setup size: 380721967 from total of 390721968 (with 10000001 hidden)
	IDE disk: Model (SAMSUNG SP2004C) serial # (S07GJ1ULC07896)
	
	Sector 0 is first sector with printable text
	============= Start text =============
	00000/000/01 00000000000033333333333333333333333333333333333333
	33333333333333333333333333333333333333333333333333333333333333333
	33333333333333333333333333333333333333333333333333333333333333333
	33333333333333333333333333333333333333333333333333333333333333333
	33333333333333333333333333333333333333333333333333333333333333333
	33333333333333333333333333333333333333333333333333333333333333333
	33333333333333333333333333333333333333333333333333333333333333333
	33333333333333333333333333333333333333333333333333333333333333333
	333333333333333333333333333333333
	============= End text Sector 0 =============
	9 <new line> characters inserted for readability
	
	Totals for all sectors
	summary format: <count> <hex value> <(actual character if printable)> ...
	  380721967 00 380721967 20 ( ) 761443934 2F (/)
	 2196468174 30 (0) 1065666422 31 (1) 897239889 32 (2)
	185762461283 33 (3) 633593182 34 (4) 624635320 35 (5)
	  580892629 36 (6) 555053801 37 (7) 545751333 38 (8)
	  544997203 39 (9)
	Totals for non-ASCII sectors
	summary format: <count> <hex value> <(actual character if printable)> ...
	
	194929647104 bytes, 380721967 sectors, 13 distinct values seen
	380721967 sectors have printable text

Tool Settings:	passes: single option: unchanged
Log Highlights:	Size after tool runs: 380721967 from total of 390721968 (with 10000001 hidden) Analysis of tool result -- Sector 380721967 is first sector with printable text ============= Start text ============= 23698/215/53 00038072196733333333333333333333333333333333333333 33333333333333333333333333333333333333333333333333333333333333333 33333333333333333333333333333333333333333333333333333333333333333 33333333333333333333333333333333333333333333333333333333333333333 33333333333333333333333333333333333333333333333333333333333333333 33333333333333333333333333333333333333333333333333333333333333333 33333333333333333333333333333333333333333333333333333333333333333 33333333333333333333333333333333333333333333333333333333333333333 333333333333333333333333333333333

```
            ============= End text Sector 380721967 =============
            9 <new line> characters inserted for readability

            Totals for all sectors
            summary format: <count> <hex value> <(actual character if printable)> ...
            194939647105 00          10000001 20 ( )       20000002 2F (/)
               49243668 30 (0)       19545260 31 (1)       27640141 32 (2)
             4889035762 33 (3)       18858011 34 (4)       13460567 35 (5)
               12330525 36 (6)       13283569 37 (7)       22563501 38 (8)
               14039504 39 (9)
            Totals for non-ASCII sectors
            summary format: <count> <hex value> <(actual character if printable)> ...
            194929647104 00

            200049647616 bytes, 390721968 sectors, 13 distinct values seen
            10000001 sectors have printable text


               Runs of Sectors Unchanged or Overwritten
            First Sector      Last Sector       State
                       0 --     380721966    Overwritten
               380721967 --     390721967    Unchanged
```

	Assertion & Expected Result	Actual Result	
Results:	FMP-CA-01 Visible sectors overwritten	as expected	
	FMP-AO-01 Hidden sectors overwritten	DCO not overwritten	
	FMP-AO-02 Hidden area final state is	in place	
Analysis:	Expected results not achieved		

1.6.5 FMP-03-DCO-HPA

Test Case FMP-03-DCO-HPA Tableau TDW1 F/W version: 04/07/10 18:21:33	
Case Summary:	FMP-03. Overwrite hidden sectors using WRITE commands.
Assertions:	FMP-CA-01 All visible sectors shall be overwritten with the specified benign data. FMP-AO-01 If there is a hidden area present and the tool supports overwriting sectors contained in a hidden area, then all sectors contained in the hidden area shall be overwritten with the specified benign data. FMP-AO-02 A hidden area may optionally be removed from the storage device.
Tester Name:	jrr
Analysis host:	frank
Test host:	tdw1
Test date:	Fri May 20 15:08:00 2011
Test drive:	2C-SATA

Source Setup:	Size with DCO: 478397167 244.94 GB (10000001 sectors in DCO)
	Size with HPA: 463397167 237.26 GB (15000000 sectors in HPA)
	Initial setup size: 463397167 from total of 488397168 (with 25000001 hidden)
	IDE disk: Model (WDC WD2500AAKS-00VSA0) serial # (WD-WMART1591607)
	
	Sector 0 is first sector with printable text
	============= Start text =============
	00000/000/01 000000000000,,,,,,,,,,,,,,,,,,,,,,,,,,,,,,,,,,,,
	,,
	,,
	,,
	,,
	,,
	,,
	,,
	,,,,,,,,,,,,,,,,,,,,,,,,,,,,,
	============= End text Sector 0 =============
	9 <new line> characters inserted for readability
	
	Totals for all sectors
	summary format: <count> <hex value> <(actual character if printable)> ...
	  478397167 00 478397167 20 ( ) 232501023162 2C (,)
	  956794334 2F (/) 2679617857 30 (0) 1259613272 31 (1)
	 1171634072 32 (2) 911352304 33 (3) 882058699 34 (4)
	  792405430 35 (5) 737463672 36 (6) 705127212 37 (7)
	  694715793 38 (8) 690749363 39 (9)
	Totals for non-ASCII sectors
	summary format: <count> <hex value> <(actual character if printable)> ...
	
	244939349504 bytes, 478397167 sectors, 14 distinct values seen
	478397167 sectors have printable text

Tool Settings:	passes: multiple option: remove hidden sectors
Log Highlights:	Size after tool runs: 488397168 from total of 488397168 (with 0 hidden) Analysis of tool result -- Totals for all sectors summary format: <count> <hex value> <(actual character if printable)> ... 250059350016 00 Totals for non-ASCII sectors summary format: <count> <hex value> <(actual character if printable)> ... 250059350016 00 250059350016 bytes, 488397168 sectors, 1 distinct values seen No sectors have printable text Runs of Sectors Unchanged or Overwritten

```
Test Case FMP-03-DCO-HPA Tableau TDW1 F/W version: 04/07/10 18:21:33
```

	First Sector	Last Sector	State	
	0 --	488397167	Overwritten	

Results:	Assertion & Expected Result	Actual Result	
	FMP-CA-01 Visible sectors overwritten	as expected	
	FMP-AO-01 Hidden sectors overwritten	as expected	
	FMP-AO-02 Hidden area final state is	removed	
Analysis:	Expected results achieved		

1.6.6 FMP-03-DCO-HPA-2

Test Case FMP-03-DCO-HPA-2 Tableau TDW1 F/W version: 04/07/10 18:21:33	
Case Summary:	FMP-03. Overwrite hidden sectors using WRITE commands.
Assertions:	FMP-CA-01 All visible sectors shall be overwritten with the specified benign data. FMP-AO-01 If there is a hidden area present and the tool supports overwriting sectors contained in a hidden area, then all sectors contained in the hidden area shall be overwritten with the specified benign data. FMP-AO-02 A hidden area may optionally be removed from the storage device.
Tester Name:	jrr
Analysis host:	frank
Test host:	tdw1
Test date:	Tue May 24 09:10:07 2011
Test drive:	1D-LAP

Source Setup:	Size with DCO: 224441647 114.91 GB (10000001 sectors in DCO)
	Size with HPA: 209441647 107.23 GB (15000000 sectors in HPA)
	Initial setup size: 209441647 from total of 234441648 (with 25000001 hidden)
	IDE disk: Model (Hitachi HTS542512K9SA00) serial # (080914BB6200WBKPDL2G)
	
	Sector 0 is first sector with printable text
	============= Start text =============
	00000/000/01 000000000000
	============= End text Sector 0 =============
	1 <new line> character inserted for readability
	
	Totals for all sectors
	summary format: <count> <hex value> <(actual character if printable)> ...
	  224441647 00 109078640442 1D 224441647 20 ( )
	  448883294 2F (/) 1412016103 30 (0) 648943728 31 (1)
	  464424108 32 (2) 386665413 33 (3) 366881139 34 (4)
	  361115513 35 (5) 335339465 36 (6) 320942104 37 (7)
	  320928507 38 (8) 320460154 39 (9)
	Totals for non-ASCII sectors
	summary format: <count> <hex value> <(actual character if printable)> ...
	
	114914123264 bytes, 224441647 sectors, 14 distinct values seen
	224441647 sectors have printable text

Tool Settings:	passes: multiple option: unchanged

Log Highlights:	Size after tool runs: 209441647 from total of 234441648 (with 25000001 hidden)
	Analysis of tool result --
	
	Sector 209441647 is first sector with printable text
	============= Start text =============
	13037/035/38 000209441647
	============= End text Sector 209441647 =============
	1 <new line> character inserted for readability
	
	Totals for all sectors
	summary format: <count> <hex value> <(actual character if printable)> ...
	107259123265 00 12150000486 1D 25000001 20 ( )
	  50000002 2F (/) 122338521 30 (0) 83167540 31 (1)
	  78756279 32 (2) 58310010 33 (3) 47086436 34 (4)
	  36417643 35 (5) 32047437 36 (6) 30473956 37 (7)
	  30475631 38 (8) 30926569 39 (9)
	Totals for non-ASCII sectors
	summary format: <count> <hex value> <(actual character if printable)> ...
	107234123264 00
	
	120034123776 bytes, 234441648 sectors, 14 distinct values seen

Test Case FMP-03-DCO-HPA-2 Tableau TDW1 F/W version: 04/07/10 18:21:33		

	25000001 sectors have printable text
	
	Runs of Sectors Unchanged or Overwritten
	First Sector Last Sector State
	         0 -- 209441646 Overwritten
	  209441647 -- 234441647 Unchanged		

Results:	**Assertion & Expected Result**	**Actual Result**
	FMP-CA-01 Visible sectors overwritten	as expected
	FMP-AO-01 Hidden sectors overwritten	DCO+HPA not overwritten
	FMP-AO-02 Hidden area final state is	in place
Analysis:	Expected results not achieved	

1.6.7 FMP-03-HPA

Test Case FMP-03-HPA Tableau TDW1 F/W version: 04/07/10 18:21:33	
Case Summary:	FMP-03. Overwrite hidden sectors using WRITE commands.
Assertions:	FMP-CA-01 All visible sectors shall be overwritten with the specified benign data. FMP-AO-01 If there is a hidden area present and the tool supports overwriting sectors contained in a hidden area, then all sectors contained in the hidden area shall be overwritten with the specified benign data. FMP-AO-02 A hidden area may optionally be removed from the storage device.
Tester Name:	jrr
Analysis host:	frank
Test host:	tdw1
Test date:	Wed May 25 10:38:33 2011
Test drive:	32-SATA

Source Setup:	Size with HPA: 141301487 72.35 GB (15000001 sectors in HPA)
	Initial setup size: 141301487 from total of 156301488 (with 15000001 hidden)
	IDE disk: Model (Hitachi HDS721680PLA380) serial # (PVF804Z31NKPSN)
	
	Sector 0 is first sector with printable text
	============= Start text =============
	00000/000/01 000000000000222222222222222222222222222222222222
	222222222222222222222222222222222222222222222222222222222222
	222222222222222222222222222222222222222222222222222222222222
	222222222222222222222222222222222222222222222222222222222222
	222222222222222222222222222222222222222222222222222222222222
	222222222222222222222222222222222222222222222222222222222222
	222222222222222222222222222222222222222222222222222222222222
	222222222222222222222222222222222222222222222222222222222222
	222222222222222222222222222222
	============= End text Sector 0 =============
	9 <new line> characters inserted for readability
	
	Totals for all sectors
	summary format: <count> <hex value> <(actual character if printable)> ...
	  156301488 00 156301488 20 ( ) 312602976 2F (/)
	  1051401436 30 (0) 387451758 31 (1) 76266080273 32 (2)
	  269597920 33 (3) 267115444 34 (4) 259739282 35 (5)
	  234788791 36 (6) 223427887 37 (7) 222956329 38 (8)
	  218596784 39 (9)
	Totals for non-ASCII sectors
	summary format: <count> <hex value> <(actual character if printable)> ...
	
	80026361856 bytes, 156301488 sectors, 13 distinct values seen
	156301488 sectors have printable text

Tool Settings:	passes: single option: remove hidden sectors
Log Highlights:	Size after tool runs: 156301488 from total of 156301488 (with 0 hidden) Analysis of tool result -- Totals for all sectors summary format: <count> <hex value> <(actual character if printable)> ... 80026361856 00 Totals for non-ASCII sectors summary format: <count> <hex value> <(actual character if printable)> ... 80026361856 00 80026361856 bytes, 156301488 sectors, 1 distinct values seen No sectors have printable text Runs of Sectors Unchanged or Overwritten First Sector Last Sector State

Test Case FMP-03-HPA Tableau TDW1 F/W version: 04/07/10 18:21:33		
	0 -- 156301487 Overwritten	
Results:	**Assertion & Expected Result**	**Actual Result**
	FMP-CA-01 Visible sectors overwritten	as expected
	FMP-AO-01 Hidden sectors overwritten	as expected
	FMP-AO-02 Hidden area final state is	removed
Analysis:	Expected results achieved	

1.6.8 FMP-03-HPA-2

Test Case FMP-03-HPA-2 Tableau TDW1 F/W version: 04/07/10 18:21:33	
Case Summary:	FMP-03. Overwrite hidden sectors using WRITE commands.
Assertions:	FMP-CA-01 All visible sectors shall be overwritten with the specified benign data. FMP-AO-01 If there is a hidden area present and the tool supports overwriting sectors contained in a hidden area, then all sectors contained in the hidden area shall be overwritten with the specified benign data. FMP-AO-02 A hidden area may optionally be removed from the storage device.
Tester Name:	jrr
Analysis host:	frank
Test host:	tdw1
Test date:	Thu May 26 09:09:49 2011
Test drive:	1C-SATA

Source Setup:	Size with HPA: 375721967 192.37 GB (15000001 sectors in HPA)
	Initial setup size: 375721967 from total of 390721968 (with 15000001 hidden)
	IDE disk: Model (Hitachi HTS722020K9SA00) serial # (080703DP04A0DTGL80TC)
	
	Sector 0 is first sector with printable text
	============= Start text =============
	00000/000/01 000000000000
	============= End text Sector 0 =============
	1 \<new line\> character inserted for readability
	
	Totals for all sectors
	summary format: \<count\> \<hex value\> \<(actual character if printable)\> ...
	  390721968 00 189890876448 1C 390721968 20 ( )
	  781443936 2F (/) 2245711842 30 (0) 1085211682 31 (1)
	  924880030 32 (2) 760620597 33 (3) 652451193 34 (4)
	  638095887 35 (5) 593223154 36 (6) 568337370 37 (7)
	  568314834 38 (8) 559036707 39 (9)
	Totals for non-ASCII sectors
	summary format: \<count\> \<hex value\> \<(actual character if printable)\> ...
	
	200049647616 bytes, 390721968 sectors, 14 distinct values seen
	390721968 sectors have printable text

Tool Settings:	passes: single option: unchanged

Log Highlights:	Size after tool runs: 375721967 from total of 390721968 (with 15000001 hidden)
	Analysis of tool result --
	
	Sector 375721967 is first sector with printable text
	============= Start text =============
	23387/155/48 000375721967
	============= End text Sector 375721967 =============
	1 \<new line\> character inserted for readability
	
	Totals for all sectors
	summary format: \<count\> \<hex value\> \<(actual character if printable)\> ...
	192384647105 00 7290000486 1C 15000001 20 ( )
	  30000002 2F (/) 73193592 30 (0) 27934472 31 (1)
	  40145510 32 (2) 45661065 33 (3) 26811904 34 (4)
	  21575209 35 (5) 20574800 36 (6) 23906703 37 (7)
	  29676297 38 (8) 20520470 39 (9)
	Totals for non-ASCII sectors
	summary format: \<count\> \<hex value\> \<(actual character if printable)\> ...
	192369647104 00
	
	200049647616 bytes, 390721968 sectors, 14 distinct values seen
	15000001 sectors have printable text

```
Test Case FMP-03-HPA-2 Tableau TDW1 F/W version: 04/07/10 18:21:33
```

	Runs of Sectors Unchanged or Overwritten First Sector Last Sector State 0 -- 375721966 Overwritten 375721967 -- 390721967 Unchanged

Results:	**Assertion & Expected Result**	**Actual Result**
	FMP-CA-01 Visible sectors overwritten	as expected
	FMP-AO-01 Hidden sectors overwritten	HPA not overwritten
	FMP-AO-02 Hidden area final state is	in place
Analysis:	Expected results not achieved	

About the National Institute of Justice

A component of the Office of Justice Programs, NIJ is the research, development and evaluation agency of the U.S. Department of Justice. NIJ's mission is to advance scientific research, development and evaluation to enhance the administration of justice and public safety. NIJ's principal authorities are derived from the Omnibus Crime Control and Safe Streets Act of 1968, as amended (see 42 U.S.C. §§ 3721–3723).

The NIJ Director is appointed by the President and confirmed by the Senate. The Director establishes the Institute's objectives, guided by the priorities of the Office of Justice Programs, the U.S. Department of Justice, and the needs of the field. The Institute actively solicits the views of criminal justice and other professionals and researchers to inform its search for the knowledge and tools to guide policy and practice.

Strategic Goals

NIJ has seven strategic goals grouped into three categories:

Creating relevant knowledge and tools

1. Partner with state and local practitioners and policymakers to identify social science research and technology needs.
2. Create scientific, relevant, and reliable knowledge—with a particular emphasis on terrorism, violent crime, drugs and crime, cost-effectiveness, and community-based efforts—to enhance the administration of justice and public safety.
3. Develop affordable and effective tools and technologies to enhance the administration of justice and public safety.

Dissemination

4. Disseminate relevant knowledge and information to practitioners and policymakers in an understandable, timely and concise manner.
5. Act as an honest broker to identify the information, tools and technologies that respond to the needs of stakeholders.

Agency management

6. Practice fairness and openness in the research and development process.
7. Ensure professionalism, excellence, accountability, cost-effectiveness and integrity in the management and conduct of NIJ activities and programs.

Program Areas

In addressing these strategic challenges, the Institute is involved in the following program areas: crime control and prevention, including policing; drugs and crime; justice systems and offender behavior, including corrections; violence and victimization; communications and information technologies; critical incident response; investigative and forensic sciences, including DNA; less-than-lethal technologies; officer protection; education and training technologies; testing and standards; technology assistance to law enforcement and corrections agencies; field testing of promising programs; and international crime control.

In addition to sponsoring research and development and technology assistance, NIJ evaluates programs, policies, and technologies. NIJ communicates its research and evaluation findings through conferences and print and electronic media.

To find out more about the National Institute of Justice, please visit:

www.nij.gov

or contact:

National Criminal Justice
 Reference Service
P.O. Box 6000
Rockville, MD 20849–6000
800–851–3420
http://www.ncjrs.gov